WHAT'S SO SCARY ABOUT
SNAKES

Joanne Mattern

RED
CHAIR
•PRESS•

What's So Scary is produced and published by Red Chair Press:

Red Chair Press LLC   PO Box 333   South Egremont, MA 01258-0333

www.redchairpress.com

 FREE Educator Guides at www.redchairpress.com/free-resources

Publisher's Cataloging-In-Publication Data

Names: Mattern, Joanne, 1963- author. | Mattern, Joanne, 1963- Earth's
    amazing animals.

Title: What's so scary about snakes? / Joanne Mattern.

Description: South Egremont, MA : Red Chair Press, [2022] | Series: Core
    content science : Earth's amazing animals | Interest age level:
    008-010. | Includes index and suggested resources for further reading.
    | Summary: "Young readers will learn the truth about the many different
    kinds of snakes, how to tell which ones are truly dangerous and which
    ones just want to be left alone, and explore up close the unique bodies
    that help these reptiles survive"--Provided by publisher.

Identifiers: ISBN 9781643711669 (hardcover) | ISBN 9781643711706
    (softcover) | ISBN 9781643711744 (ePDF) | ISBN 9781643711782 (ePub 3
    S&L) | ISBN 9781643711829 (ePub 3 TR) | ISBN 9781643711867 (Kindle)

Subjects: LCSH: Snakes--Juvenile literature. | CYAC: Snakes.

Classification: LCC QL666.O6 M38 2022 (print) | LCC QL666.O6 (ebook) | DDC
    597.96--dc23

Library of Congress Control Number: 2021945360

Photo credits: iStock

Printed in United States of America
0422 1P CGF22

Table of Contents

Scary Snakes!

A dark shape slithers out from under a rock. It uncoils its long, powerful body and moves toward you. Then, before you can run away, its sharp fangs strike. This snake is on the attack!

Many people are scared of snakes. It's true that some snakes are scary. Some are **venomous**. They can kill with one bite of their fangs. Other snakes are super-strong. They can squeeze the life right out of their **prey**.

But most snakes won't hurt you. Snakes are amazing animals. They are important **predators** that play a big role in life on Earth. Let's learn more about snakes and why most of them are not so scary.

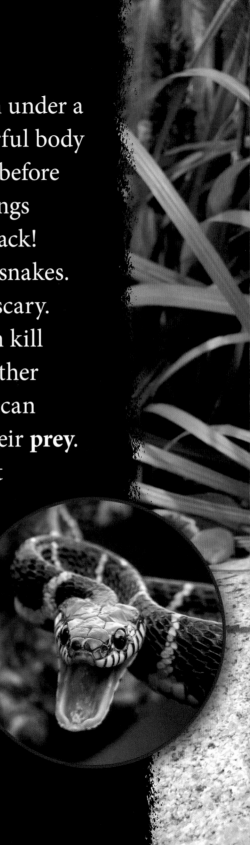

Snake Basics

Snakes are reptiles. Like all reptiles, snakes are cold-blooded. That means they cannot control their body temperature. Reptile bodies are covered with hard scales. They do not have fur or hair. Most reptiles lay eggs instead of giving birth to babies.

There are more than 3,000 **species** of snakes. They live in most parts of the world. The only places snakes do not live are Antarctica, Ireland, New Zealand, Iceland, and Greenland. Most snakes live on land, but some live in the ocean.

Now You Know!

Other members of the reptile family are lizards, alligators, crocodiles, turtles and tortoises, and tuataras.

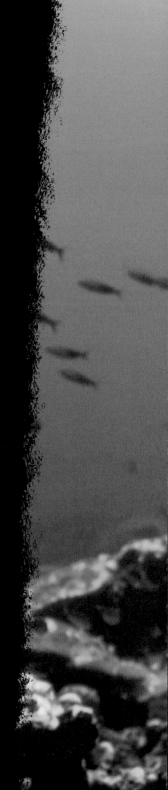

The Black-banded sea snake is 10-times stronger than a cobra. Like this one in Indonesia, they hunt fish hiding in coral reefs.

Snake Bodies

Snakes do not have arms or legs. They move by stretching and tightening their muscles. A snake's body has more than 200 **vertebrae**. They also have up to 400 ribs. These small bones help protect the snake's body.

Snakes come in many different sizes. The giant anaconda can weigh up to 550 pounds (250 kg.) and is more than 17 feet (more than 5 m.) long. The longest snake is the reticulated python. It can be up to 30 feet (9 m.) long.

Now You Know!

The Barbados thread snake is the world's smallest snake. It is only about four inches (10 cm.) long. This snake eats tiny insects. That's not so scary!

The reticulated python
is the longest snake.

Snake Senses

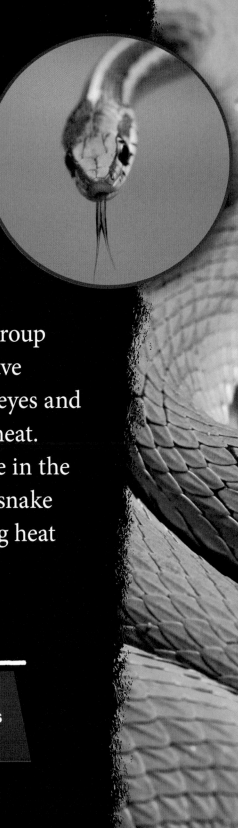

Snakes can't see or hear very well. But they have a very strong sense of smell. Snakes flick their tongues out to catch animal smells nearby. This helps them find prey to eat.

Some snakes belong to a group called pit vipers. Pit vipers have special organs between their eyes and mouth. These pits can sense heat. They are connected to a nerve in the snake's eyes. That means the snake can actually "see" heat. Seeing heat helps snakes find their prey.

Now You Know!

Snakes can also feel vibrations in the ground. They feel them through bones in their jaws.

Large-eyed green pit viper of Southeast Asia. Don't let its beautiful color fool you!

Snakes swallow their prey whole. Some snakes can even swallow animals that are much bigger than they are, like deer or pigs. A snake's jaws are very loose. They can stretch far apart. The snake pulls its prey into its mouth. Then muscles in its body pull the prey into the snake's stomach.

Now You Know!

After it eats a large meal, a snake does not have to eat again for several months.

Garter snake after eating an insect

This venomous Bush viper snake is swallowing a rodent.

Striking and Squeezing

All snakes are **carnivores**. They hunt other animals for food. Snakes can be divided into two groups.

Many snakes are **constrictors**. These snakes kill their prey by squeezing it. A constrictor wraps its body around its prey. It uses its powerful muscles to squeeze until the prey stops breathing. Pythons, boa constrictors, and king snakes are all constrictors.

Other snakes use their long fangs to catch and kill their prey. Some of these snakes are venomous. Their fangs inject **venom** into their prey. Venom can make the prey's heart stop or keep it from breathing. Rattlesnakes, cottonmouths, copperheads, and coral snakes are all venomous snakes that live in the United States.

Baby Snakes

Almost all snakes lay eggs. A female snake can lay more than 30 soft eggs at a time. She hides them in a safe place, like a hole in a tree. Then she leaves. The babies hatch about 60 days later.

Baby snakes can take care of themselves as soon as they are born. As they grow, their skin gets too tight. When that happens, the snake sheds its skin. A new, bigger skin grows in its place.

Now You Know!

Boa constrictors, sea snakes, and pythons give birth to live young.

Corn snake hatchlings.
This type of rat snake,
lives in the U.S.

Meet the Snakes

Here are a few of the many species of snakes on Planet Earth:

Reticulated Python

This huge snake lives in the rainforests of Southeast Asia. It likes to hang from trees and wait for prey to pass by. Then it constricts its prey until its dead. Reticulated python moms take care of their young. They wrap their bodies around the eggs to keep them warm.

Reticulated python

Red spitting cobra

Red Spitting Cobra

This snake doesn't actually spit. It sprays its venom up to six feet away, aiming for its victim's eyes. These snakes also spread out their necks into a flat hood to look bigger and scare away enemies. Red spitting cobras live in Africa.

Copperhead

Copperhead

Copperheads live in the eastern and central United States. These large, heavy snakes often hide in piles of leaves or under rocks. This snake is venomous and eats almost anything, including, mice, frogs, lizards, birds, and insects.

Yellow-Bellied Sea Snake

This ocean-dwelling snake lives in warm waters. These snakes often float on the water in large groups. They also use their flat tail to paddle through the water. Sea snakes can stay underwater for up to three hours. They eat small fish and eels.

Yellow-bellied
sea snake

Garter Snake

Garter snakes are very common in the United States. They live almost everywhere from Florida up to Canada. These snakes are harmless to people, but some have venom that can kill small animals. Garter snakes snuggle together in huge groups to stay warm during cold weather.

Garter snake

Death Adder

The death adder is the deadliest snake in Australia. Its venom **paralyzes** its victims and usually kills them very quickly. Death adders are active at night. They like to lie still and **ambush** their prey when it walks by.

Warning! Danger Ahead!

Snakes are important to keeping life on Earth in balance. They are predators who eat many small animals. Without snakes, there would be a lot more animal pests like mice and insects.

Most snakes do not attack humans. Snakes are shy and don't want to be around people. They are not that scary.

However, some snakes do attack people. Snake attacks usually happen when a human surprises the snake or comes too close. The snake feels scared, so it strikes out at the danger.

Some snake bites can be very dangerous, others just itch for awhile.

Now You Know!

Doctors use snake venom to treat snake bites! Venom is collected from snake and injected into an animal. The animal's body forms antibodies that can fight the venom. Scientists collect those antibodies and use it to make antivenom.

Staying Safe From Snakes

The best way to stay safe from snakes is to leave them alone. Be careful if you are walking in an area where there are snakes. For example, rattlesnakes live in the desert. Copperheads are found in the woods and under rocks. Cottonmouths live near water. Be alert and look for snakes in your path. If you see one, back away and do not touch it.

Western diamondback
rattlesnakes are a very
dangerous type of viper.

Snakes in Trouble

Snakes seem scary, but the truth is that humans are a bigger danger to snakes than they are to us. Many people kill snakes because they do not like them, or they are afraid of them. Others kill snakes to make medicine from their body parts, or use their skins to make fashion items.

Boots made from rattlesnake skin are prized for lasting a very long time.

The biggest danger facing snakes is loss of **habitat**. When people cut down woods and forests, or pave over fields, they destroy the places where snakes live. They also kill the animals snakes use for food.

Now You Know!

The Saint Lucia racer is the most **endangered** snake in the world. Fewer than 20 of these snakes live on a tiny island in the Caribbean Sea.

Helping Snakes

There are lots of ways to help snakes. One of the best ways is to learn about them. Study all the amazing things snakes can do, and teach others that snakes are not that scary!

Many wildlife groups are working to save snakes around the world. They have created wildlife preserves where snakes and other animals are safe from habitat loss or hunting. Helping these organizations is a great way to save snakes and make our world a less scary place.

Glossary

ambush to attack an animal by surprise

carnivores animals that eat other animals

constrictors snakes that squeeze their prey to death

endangered in danger of dying out

habitat the place where an animal lives

paralyzes causes something to be unable to move

predators animals that hunt other animals for food

prey animals that are hunted by other animals for food

scales thin, hard plates that cover a reptile's body

species a group of living things of the same kind

venom poison that is injected into the body by a bite or a sting

venomous having venom that is given by biting or stinging something or someone

vertebrae bones that form the spine

Learn More in the Library

Blake, Kevin. *Deadly Snake Bite!* Bearport Publishing, 2019.

Bodden, Valerie. *Amazing Animals: Snakes*. Creative Education, 2020.

Kenney, Karen Latchana. *Life Cycle of a Snake*. Pogo, 2019.

Terp, Gail. *Sea Snakes*. Black Rabbit Books, 2021.

Index

About the Author

Joanne Mattern is the author of many books for children including the previous three sets of *Core Content: Earth's Amazing Animals Series.* She loves writing about sports, all kinds of animals, and interesting people. Mattern lives in New York State with her family.